Hello Jesus

"Good morning Jesus!" I say at sunrise.

With my soft teddy I gaze at the skies.

Dad and Mom give me a cuddle too.

They pick me up and say "I love you!"

The weather gives me clues of how to dress.

I look so cute. These shoes are the best.

I have lots of fun with all my toys.

Those that roll, bounce or make noise.

We walk to the park, to see my good friends.

We play, we slide, we swing. Fun never ends!

Sand fills my toy truck until it overflows.

Jesus loves me from my head to my toes.

With a stroller and a piggy-back ride,

We travel home, with Jesus by our side.

With water, bubbles and a towel that's green,

Mom gives me a bath, and now I'm all clean.

When the day is done, it's time to go to bed.

I say "Good night Jesus!" as I lay down my head.

More books from iCharacter.org

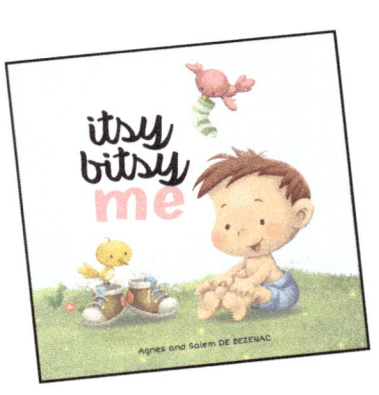

www.iCharacter.org
Published by iCharacter Ltd. (Ireland)
By Agnes and Salem de Bezenac
Illustrated by Agnes de Bezenac
Colored by Henny Y.
Copyright 2019. All rights reserved.

Copyright © 2019 by iCharacter Limited. All rights reserved. No part of this book may be reproduced in any form or by any electronic or mechanical means, including information storage and retrieval systems, without written permission from the publisher or author, except in the case of a reviewer, who may quote brief passages embodied in critical articles or in a review.

www.ingramcontent.com/pod-product-compliance
Lightning Source LLC
Chambersburg PA
CBHW040013080526
44586CB00028B/2998